Soul Soothing Scriptures

22 Coloring Pages + 22 Verses
To *Meditate* On As You *Color*

ColorThroughTheBible.com
Color Through the Bible: Volume 1

Published by CreateSpace in 2016
Third edition: Third printing

Illustrations and Cover Photo by Debbie Hannah Skinner

Head shot by Alex Karber

Cover Design by Debbie Hannah Skinner and Karen R. Power

Interior Design by Karen R. Power and Debbie Hannah Skinner

Scripture quotations marked (KJV) are taken from the Holy Bible, King James Version. Public Domain.

Scripture quotations marked (WEB) are taken from the Holy Bible, World English Bible. Public Domain.

WisdomInWatercolor.com
ColorThroughTheBible.com

ISBN-978-1-523650-16-3

To all those who love Scripture and art.

May the pages within this book
inspire you
to focus your heart on God
as you engage your hands in art.

Table of Contents

About This Coloring Book

Welcome. I am so glad you are here!

This coloring book was designed to help you. . .

- find a new sense of focus as you meditate on Scripture
- practice "intentional abiding" in God's word
- enjoy encouragement that comes from slowly savoring Scriptures, and
- cut through distractions hindering your spiritual growth

With those outcomes in mind, *Color Through The Bible, Volume 1: Soul Soothing Scriptures* is filled with 22 inspirational, framable coloring pages and 22 soul soothing Scriptures for you to ponder as you color.

I hope you'll find within the pages of this book a place to stop and find rest for your soul as you experience the anxiety-reducing joy of meditating on Scripture as you color.

-Debbie Hannah Skinner

A Simple Prayer

Dear Lord,
Please use the Scriptures
and coloring spaces in
this book to bring the
soothing peace and calm
of Your presence
into the hearts
of those taking time
to turn their
full attention toward You.
You are worthy.
Amen.

User's Guide

The Tools

Gather your coloring materials. Watercolor pencils, watercolor paints, colored pencils, markers, or pens are great choices for use in this book.

Since I'm a watercolorist, I love to use **watercolor pencils** and I hope you'll try them. With watercolor pencils, once a page is colored you can use a paintbrush and tiny bit of water to activate and blend the pigment. You can also paint with water first, then color into the water for a totally different look.

Because watercolor is a transparent pigment (as compared to acrylic and oil paint) it's great for layering color. I hope you'll give this versatile art medium a try!

Once your page dries, you can use your watercolor pencils to add other colors on top, like layers of stained glass. The colorful options are endless.

You will find a few "Play Ground" pages in back of the book where you can experiment with your art supplies and colors of choice before committing them to a coloring page.

You will find some "Play Ground" pages in back of the book where you can experiment with your art supplies and colors of choice before committing them to a coloring page.

The Time

Let's face it- everybody is busy these days. It takes effort to make space in your schedule for coloring, but I hope you discover that coloring is one of the most relaxing and releasing activities you can take part in for the benefit of your soul.

Carve out a bit of time for contemplative coloring in your schedule.

Make a coloring appointment with yourself and put it on your calendar.

I've taken my portable coloring tools to coffee shops, city parks, beside a lake, and even on an airplane. You can color just about any place once you decide to set aside the time to do it.

A Simple Technique

Ingest
(Read a Scripture verse)

Digest
(Ponder the meaning)

Write the verse
(On your coloring page)

Rest
(Meditate on the verse as you color)

Step 1: Ingest A Scripture Verse

The Bible is absolutely loaded with encouraging words that can soothe your soul. Before you dive into coloring, I invite you to first dig into Scripture to look intently at the verse provided to accompany each coloring sheet.

Right before each coloring page, you'll find a Bible verse from two translations- the King James Version (KJV) and the World English Bible (WEB). These are older, public domain versions written in powerful, poetic language.

If you'd prefer to use a more modern translation of the verse, you'll also find a space where you can write that same verse from a different translation of your choice.

Once you compare the various translation of the verse, select the one you want to focus on as you're coloring.

"Let the word of Christ dwell in you richly. . ."
Colossians 3:16a

Step 2: Digest The Verse Using The "Pause To Ponder" Page

On the back of the Bible verse page, you'll find a "Pause to Ponder" page with space to think about that particular verse by **doodling** or **drawing** or **writing**.

Think of the "Pause to Ponder" page as a place for visual journaling of your thoughts and impressions in preparation for your time of contemplative coloring.

Using simple key word prompts. . .

Who?

What?

When?

Where?

Why?

How?

What if?

. . . this page is where you can spend time thinking about how the verse connects with your life right now. There's no pressure to respond to all of the key word prompts. Use as few or as many as you'd like.

Doodle or draw or write your thoughts about the connections you see. If other related or similar Bible verses come to mind, write them in this space as well.

Step 3: Write The Verse On Your Coloring Page

You'll notice one large blank space on all of the coloring sheets. That's your "Scripture space" where you'll copy the verse you plan to contemplate as you color. (I typically write the verse using a black pen.)

> **You can mix and match coloring pages with the verses any way you'd like.** ☺

Why Write The Scripture?

There is tremendous value in writing Scripture. You can even see this in the Bible.

In the Old Testament, the Israelites were on the verge of entering the Promised Land after spending over 400 years in Egypt. Through Moses, the LORD instructed them on how they were to relate to Him and to each other as they entered in to possess this new territory.

In the book of Deuteronomy, the LORD tells His people, through Moses, a day was coming when the people of Israel would have a king of their own. In Deuteronomy 17, special instructions were given in regard to how the king was to interact with God's Law...

> **18 It shall be, when he sits on the throne of his kingdom, that he shall write himself a copy of this law in a book, out of that which is before the priests the Levites. 19 It shall be with him, and he shall read from it all the days of his life; that he may learn to fear Yahweh his God, to keep all the words of this law and these statutes, to do them; 20 that his heart not be lifted up above his brothers, and that he not turn aside from the commandment, to the right hand, or to the left; to the end that he may prolong his days in his kingdom, he and his children, in the middle of Israel. Deuteronomy 17:18-20 WEB**

"He shall write himself a copy."

Isn't it interesting that God did not instruct the king to simply read a copy of the law passed down from his ancestors, written by someone else's hand? The king isn't told to ask his royal secretary to create a copy on his behalf. Instead, God commanded the king to interact with the word of God in a personal, private, and direct way—through writing.

The LORD, in His vast wisdom, instructed the king to look at the words of the law, to think about them, and then to transfer them accurately to a scroll—in his own handwriting—because of specific benefits he would receive.

Matthew Henry said the following about Deuteronomy 17:18 in *Matthew Henry's Commentary on the Whole Bible: Complete and Unabridged in One Volume*:

> "Though he had secretaries about him whom he might employ to write this copy, and who perhaps could write a better hand than he, yet he must do it himself, with his own hand, for the honour of the law, and that he might think no act of religion below him, to inure himself to labour and study, and especially that he might thereby be obliged to take particular notice of every part of the law and by writing it might imprint it in his mind."

This written internalization of God's word would help the king revere God, follow God's commands, keep him humble in relation to his brothers, and help him to not turn from the law.

Likewise, as we take the time to write Scripture today, we can experience similar beautiful benefits as well.

The act of writing can help us retain information, increase our ability to focus, and cut through distractions. For many people, it's a super effective way to learn.

Engaging your hands
in doodling or writing or coloring or painting
is a powerful way
to be present in the moment
and focus undivided attention
on the LORD.

Writing Bible verses can help us comprehend God's word in a more complete, clear, and intimate way. Scriptures copied by our own hand are often more fresh on the mind and close to the heart, as well.

One additional benefit of writing Scripture is accuracy.

Have you ever found yourself vaguely familiar with a certain Bible verse, only to discover your paraphrase is incorrect? It's easy to leave out key words or concepts, but writing the verse can prevent this.

If you're a "skim reader" (like me), the practice of writing Bible verses can help you take note of every important component of Scripture.

Once your translation is selected and the verse is written on your coloring page, you're ready for the final step: contemplative coloring.

"A prudent pen may go far towards making up the deficiencies of the memory, and the furnishings of the treasures of the good householder with things new and old..." - Matthew Henry

Step 4: Meditate On The Verse As You Color

Meditation is mentioned fourteen times in the Old Testament. Interestingly, the Hebrew word for meditate, *siyach*, has a very precise meaning.

According to *Biblesoft's New Exhaustive Strong's Numbers and Concordance with Expanded Greek-Hebrew Dictionary*, meditate means "to ponder, i.e. (by implication) converse (with oneself, and hence, aloud) or utter."

Do you ever talk aloud to yourself? According to this definition, that's a form of meditation, but Biblical meditation is even more.

The <u>object</u> of meditation in the Old Testament is God— His works and His ways and His word.

Many people think of meditation as the *emptying* of the mind, but Biblical meditation is actually a *filling* of the mind—with thoughts of the LORD and His word.

As you fill your mind with the remembrance of God's word, saying the words over and over to yourself (whether silently or aloud), you are practicing the Biblical meaning meditation.

Slowly Savor the Scripture

The Chocolate Experiment

I love the taste of milk chocolate. When I place a small piece of chocolate in my mouth, I have a choice to make. I can eat it quickly or make my chocolate experience last as long as possible.

Often, I let the chocolate slowly melt in my mouth. (Yum. . . If you're a chocolate lover, too, you may want to find a piece and practice this!)

As it dissolves, I pay close attention to all the varied textures and flavors I notice. I ask myself, "Does it taste smooth? Bitter? Sweet? Salty? What about the texture? How does it feel?" This approach has helped me learn that not all chocolate is the same.

Taking time to slowly get the most out of the taste of the chocolate and the experience of eating it is called savoring.

We live in a hurried, hectic, fast food culture that can hinder our ability to savor if we're not careful. I recently spent an afternoon in an airport terminal, watching people rush by, inhaling food as they traveled. Boarding times, gate changes, and looming deadlines pushed people to eat on the go. I've done the same thing myself and can tell you it's a recipe for indigestion.

It's not too different in daily life, is it? We are all overly hurried. Intentionally *savoring* puts a stop to all the rushing around. It allows us to notice tiny little nuances of flavor and to be present in the moment.

Likewise, savoring Scripture as you color—meditating on each word, pondering the phrases, weighing the words, even repeating the entire verse to yourself while engaging your hands in coloring—can be a powerful spiritual practice to help you rest your mind and focus your attention on God's word in the present moment.

We can't meditate or color in the past.

We can't meditate or color in the future.

We can <u>only</u> meditate or color in the present.

This practice of contemplative coloring—meditating on God's word as you color—can help you plumb the depths of meaning in Scripture you may have previously overlooked.

Take your time.

Take it slow.

Savor the Scripture.

Color contemplatively.

My hope is that as you color while meditating on Scripture, you will experience a restful, peaceful, colorful "oasis" time in your day. This investment can bear the fruit of the beautiful picture seen in Psalm 1:1-3 in your life.

Finally, brothers,
whatever things are true,
whatever things are
honorable,
whatever things are just,
whatever things are pure,
whatever things are lovely,
whatever things are
of good report;
if there is any virtue,
and if there is any praise,
think about these things.

Philippians 4:8 (WEB)

A Few Last Thoughts

(in no particular order)

Unlike many other coloring books, these designs are intentionally simple and spacious instead of being intricate and busy. That's to give you room to layer colors and textures in the spaces.

Once you finish coloring your Scripture page, you can use a craft knife or scissors to carefully remove your page.

Consider adding a mat and/or frame to your coloring sheet.

Praying a verse for a friend, then giving them the coloring page in a mat or frame, can be a great gift of encouragement.

Display your work in your home as a way to continue to meditate on God's word after your coloring session is over.

Do you have adult children? Consider sending them a sheet you have colored to hang on *their* refrigerator. ☺

Finishing this coloring book is not winning a race. There's no prize for being the first to finish. There's also no competition here.

Finally, please remember it's about the *process* of contemplating as you color, not the *product*. Be kind to yourself and enjoy the journey of engaging your hands and your heart to meditate on Scripture.

Psalm 3:3

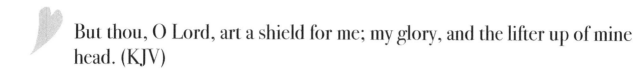

But thou, O Lord, art a shield for me; my glory, and the lifter up of mine head. (KJV)

But you, Yahweh, are a shield around me, my glory, and the one who lifts up my head. (WEB)

My Favorite Bible Translation of this Verse:

Pause to Ponder

Doodle . Draw . Write . Doodle . Draw . Write

Who?

What?

When?

Where?

Why?

How?

What if?

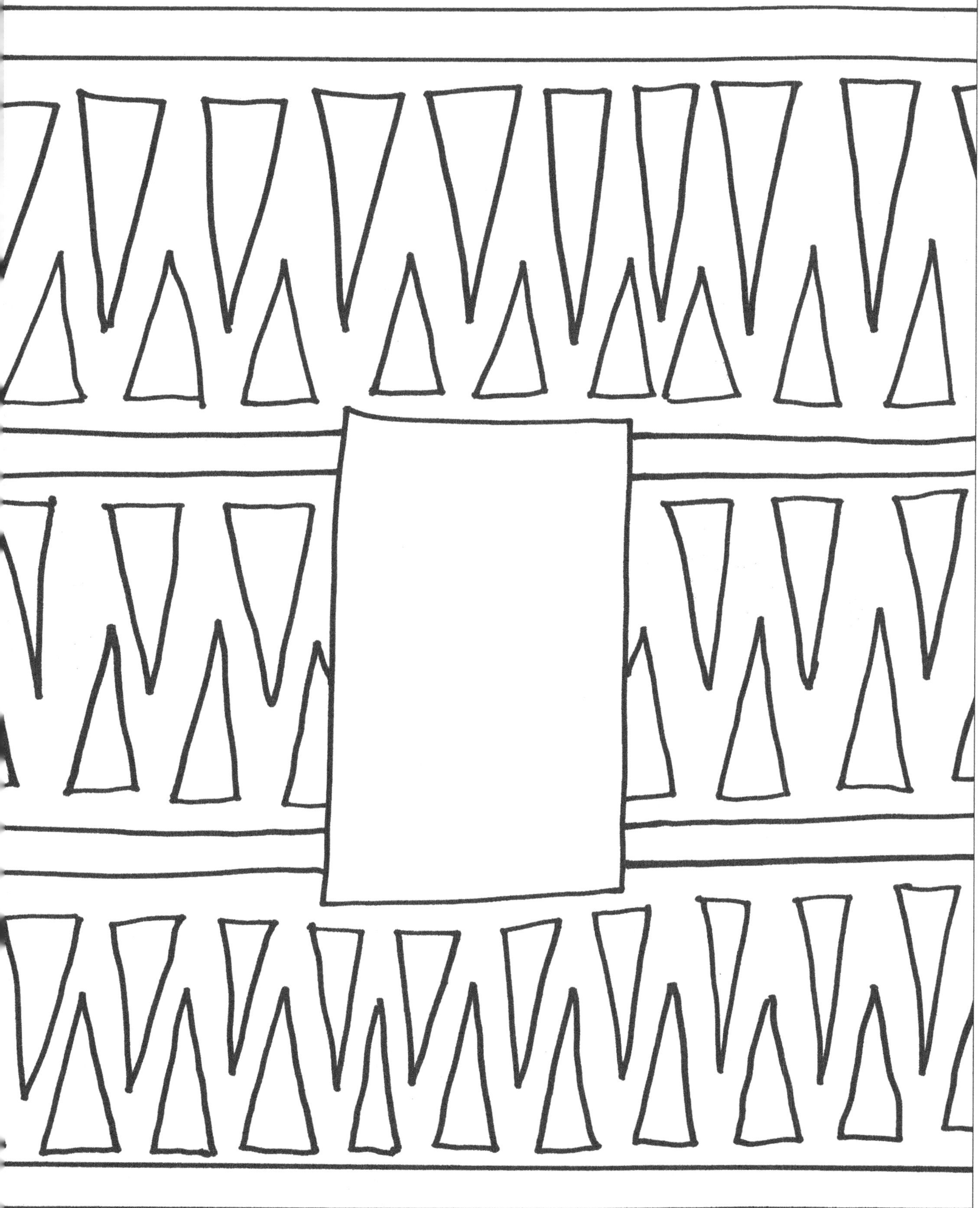

Psalm 4:8

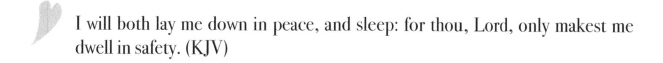

I will both lay me down in peace, and sleep: for thou, Lord, only makest me dwell in safety. (KJV)

In peace I will both lay myself down and sleep, for you, Yahweh alone, make me live in safety. (WEB)

My Favorite Bible Translation of this Verse:

Pause to Ponder

Who?

What?

When?

Where?

Why?

How?

What if?

Psalm 16:11

 Thou wilt shew me the path of life: in thy presence is fulness of joy; at thy right hand there are pleasures for evermore. (KJV)

 You will show me the path of life. In your presence is fullness of joy. In your right hand there are pleasures forever more. (WEB)

My Favorite Bible Translation of this Verse:

Pause to Ponder

Doodle . Draw . Write . Doodle . Draw . Write

Who?

What?

When?

Where?

Why?

How?

What if?

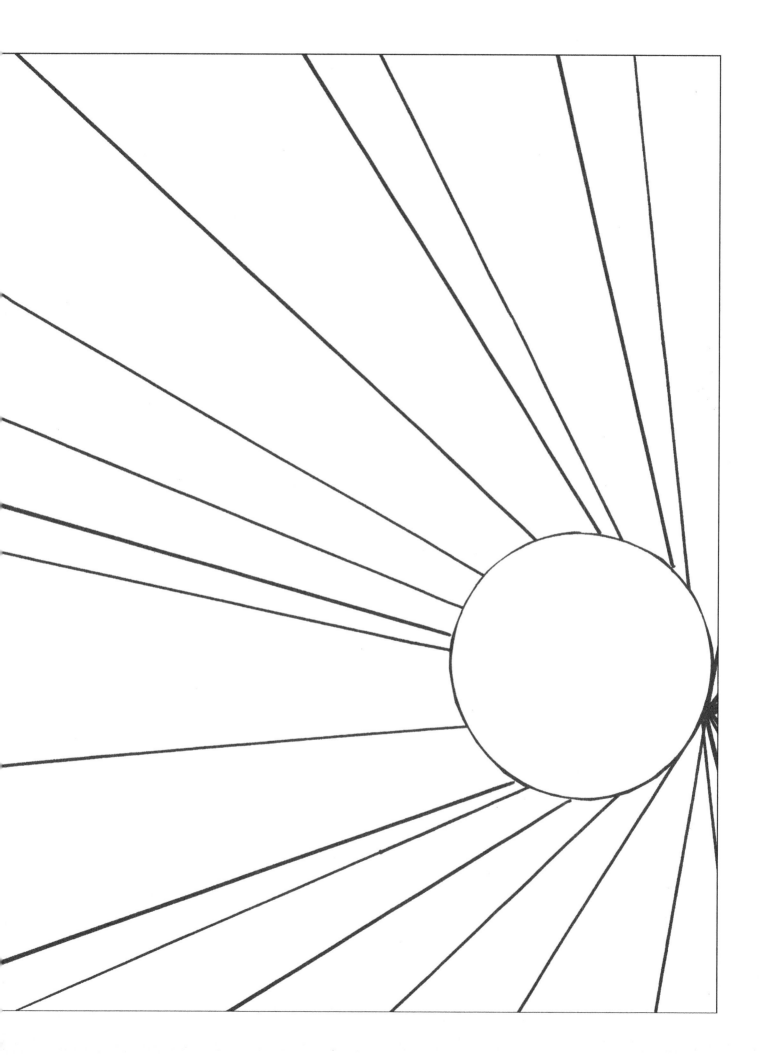

Psalm 40:11

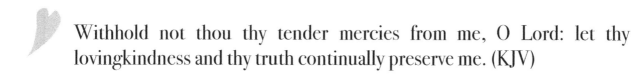 Withhold not thou thy tender mercies from me, O Lord: let thy lovingkindness and thy truth continually preserve me. (KJV)

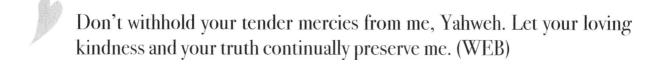 Don't withhold your tender mercies from me, Yahweh. Let your loving kindness and your truth continually preserve me. (WEB)

My Favorite Bible Translation of this Verse:

Pause to Ponder

Doodle . Draw . Write . Doodle . Draw . Write

Who?

What?

When?

Where?

Why?

How?

What if?

Psalm 42:5

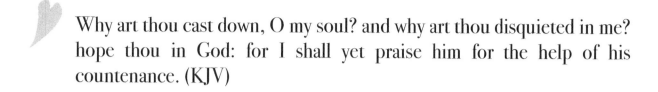

Why art thou cast down, O my soul? and why art thou disquieted in me? hope thou in God: for I shall yet praise him for the help of his countenance. (KJV)

Why are you in despair, my soul? Why are you disturbed within me? Hope in God! For I shall still praise him for the saving help of his presence. (WEB)

My Favorite Bible Translation of this Verse:

Pause to Ponder

Doodle . Draw . Write . Doodle . Draw . Write

Who?

What?

When?

Where?

Why?

How?

What if?

Psalm 46:10

Be still, and know that I am God: I will be exalted among the heathen, I will be exalted in the earth. (KJV)

Be still, and know that I am God. I will be exalted among the nations. I will be exalted in the earth. (WEB)

My Favorite Bible Translation of this Verse:

Pause to Ponder

Doodle . Draw . Write . Doodle . Draw . Write

Who?

What?

When?

Where?

Why?

How?

What if?

Psalm 55:16-17

 As for me, I will call upon God; And the Lord shall save me. Evening, and morning, and at noon, will I pray, and cry aloud: And he shall hear my voice. (KJV)

 As for me, I will call on God. Yahweh will save me. Evening, morning, and at noon, I will cry out in distress. He will hear my voice. (WEB)

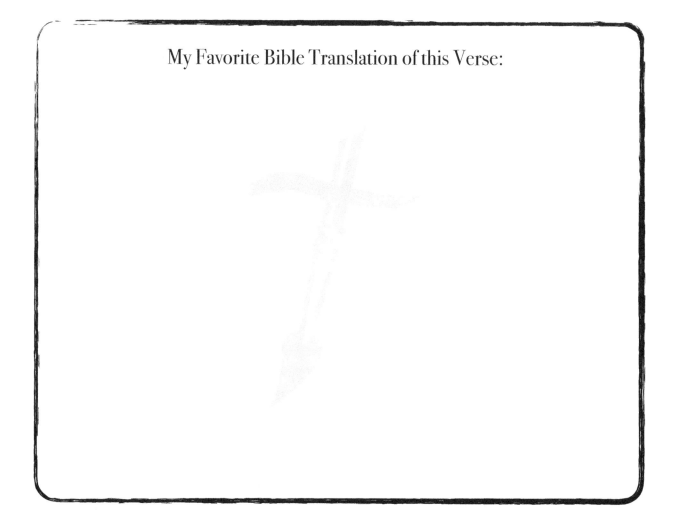

My Favorite Bible Translation of this Verse:

Pause to Ponder

Doodle . Draw . Write . Doodle . Draw . Write

Who?

What?

When?

Where?

Why?

How?

What if?

Psalm 55:22

 Cast thy burden upon the Lord, and he shall sustain thee: He shall never suffer the righteous to be moved. (KJV)

 Cast your burden on Yahweh, and he will sustain you. He will never allow the righteous to be moved. (WEB)

My Favorite Bible Translation of this Verse:

Pause to Ponder

Doodle . Draw . Write . Doodle . Draw . Write

Who?

What?

When?

Where?

Why?

How?

What if?

Psalm 73:26

My flesh and my heart faileth: But God is the strength of my heart, and my portion forever. (KJV)

My flesh and my heart fails, but God is the strength of my heart and my portion forever. (WEB)

My Favorite Bible Translation of this Verse:

Pause to Ponder

Doodle . Draw . Write . Doodle . Draw . Write

Who?

What?

When?

Where?

Why?

How?

What if?

Psalm 73:28

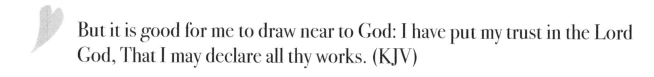

But it is good for me to draw near to God: I have put my trust in the Lord God, That I may declare all thy works. (KJV)

But it is good for me to come close to God. I have made the Lord Yahweh my refuge, that I may tell of all your works. (WEB)

My Favorite Bible Translation of this Verse:

Pause to Ponder

Doodle . Draw . Write . Doodle . Draw . Write

Who?

What?

When?

Where?

Why?

How?

What if?

Psalm 62:5-6

 My soul, wait thou only upon God; For my expectation is from him. He only is my rock and my salvation: He is my defence; I shall not be moved. (KJV)

 My soul, wait in silence for God alone, for my expectation is from him. He alone is my rock and my salvation, my fortress, will not be shaken. (WEB)

My Favorite Bible Translation of this Verse:

Pause to Ponder

Who?

What?

When?

Where?

Why?

How?

What if?

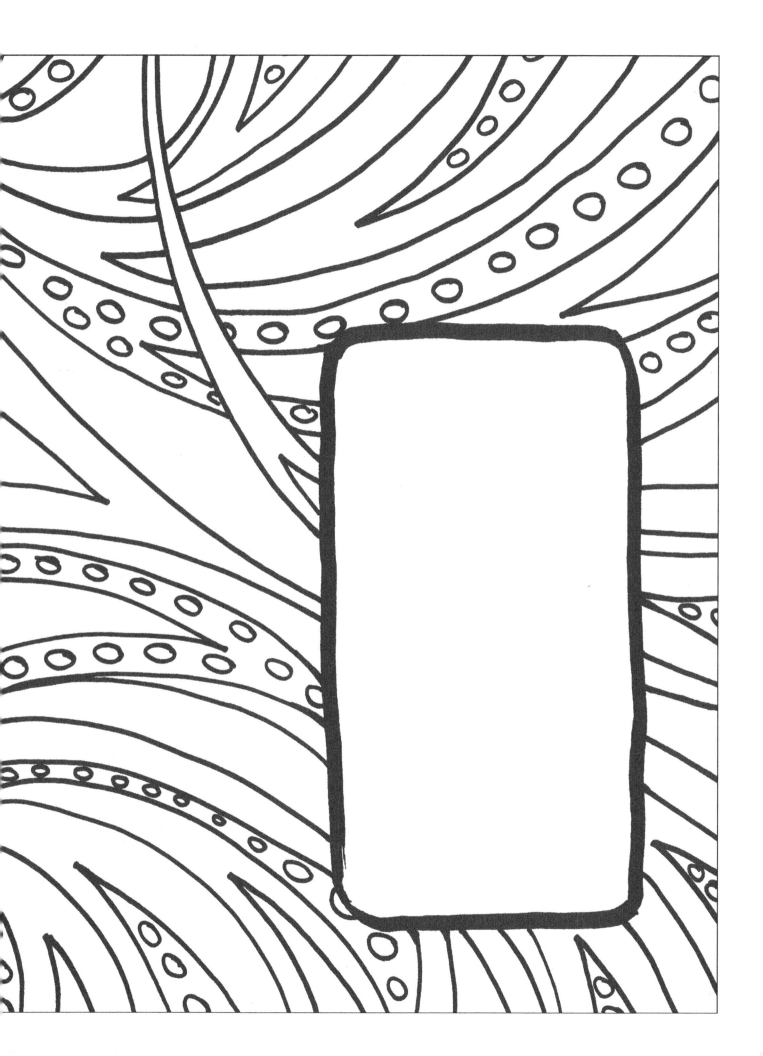

Exodus 33:14

 And he said, "My Presence shall go with thee, and I will give thee rest." (KJV)

 He said, "My presence will go with you, and I will give you rest." (WEB)

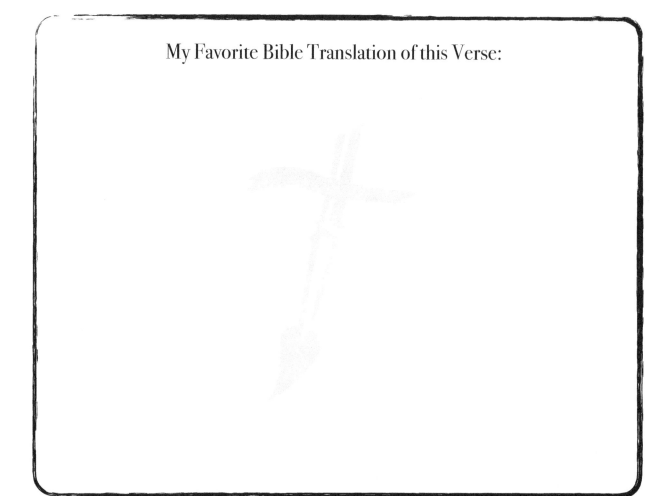

My Favorite Bible Translation of this Verse:

Pause to Ponder

Doodle . Draw . Write . Doodle . Draw . Write

Who?

What?

When?

Where?

Why?

How?

What if?

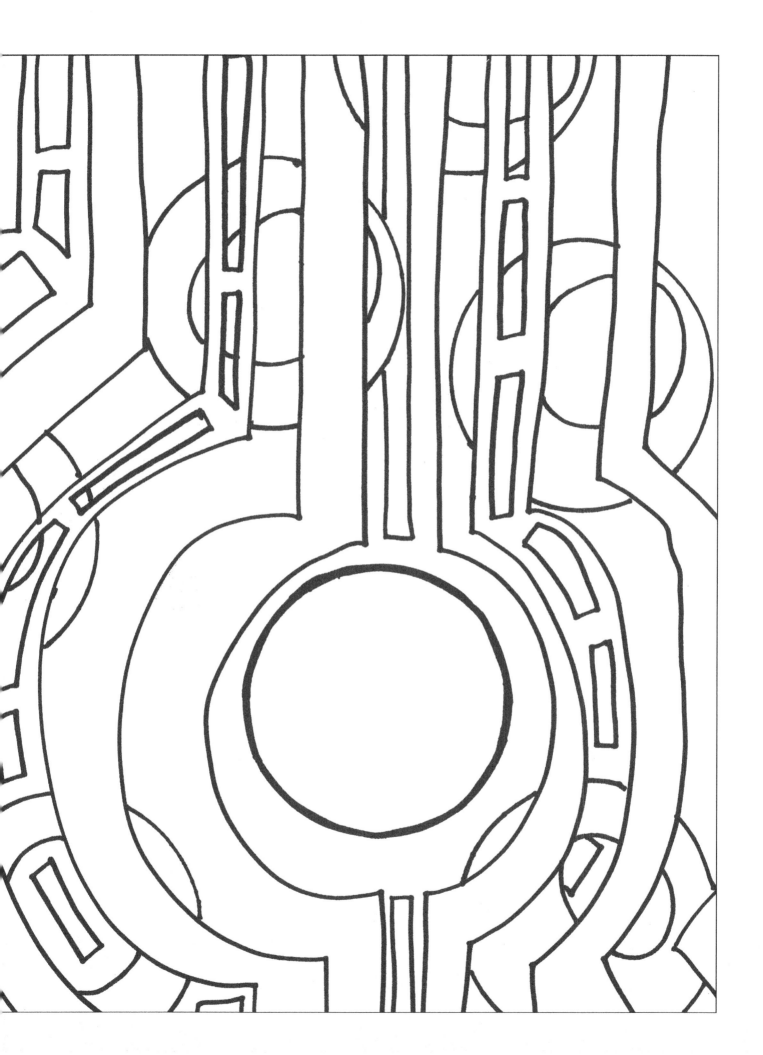

Psalm 94:19

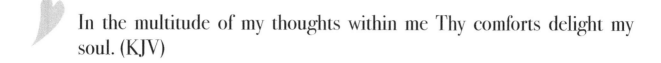

In the multitude of my thoughts within me Thy comforts delight my soul. (KJV)

In the multitude of my thoughts within me, your comforts delight my soul. (WEB)

My Favorite Bible Translation of this Verse:

Pause to Ponder

Doodle . Draw . Write . Doodle . Draw . Write

Who?

What?

When?

Where?

Why?

How?

What if?

Matthew 11:28

 Come unto me, all ye that labour and are heavy laden, and I will give you rest. (KJV)

 Come to me, all you who labor and are heavily burdened, and I will give you rest. (WEB)

My Favorite Bible Translation of this Verse:

Pause to Ponder

Doodle . Draw . Write . Doodle . Draw . Write

Who?

What?

When?

Where?

Why?

How?

What if?

John 14:27

 Peace I leave with you, my peace I give unto you: not as the world giveth, give I unto you. Let not your heart be troubled, neither let it be afraid. (KJV)

 Peace I leave with you. My peace I give to you; not as the world gives, give I to you. Don't let your heart be troubled, neither let it be fearful. (WEB)

My Favorite Bible Translation of this Verse:

Pause to Ponder

Who?

What?

When?

Where?

Why?

How?

What if?

Psalm 62:2

He only is my rock and my salvation; He is my defence; I shall not be greatly moved. (KJV)

He alone is my rock and my salvation, my fortress—I will never be greatly shaken. (WEB)

My Favorite Bible Translation of this Verse:

Pause to Ponder

Doodle . Draw . Write . Doodle . Draw . Write

Who?

What?

When?

Where?

Why?

How?

What if?

John 16:33

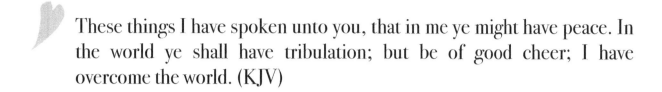

These things I have spoken unto you, that in me ye might have peace. In the world ye shall have tribulation; but be of good cheer; I have overcome the world. (KJV)

I have told you these things, that in me you may have peace. In the world you have oppression; but cheer up! I have overcome the world. (WEB)

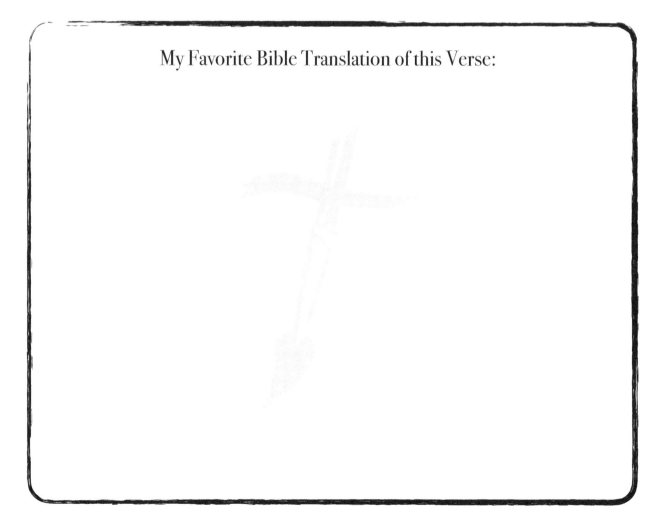

My Favorite Bible Translation of this Verse:

Pause to Ponder

Doodle . Draw . Write . Doodle . Draw . Write

Who?

What?

When?

Where?

Why?

How?

What if?

Philippians 4:6

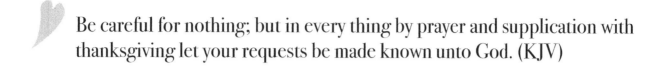

Be careful for nothing; but in every thing by prayer and supplication with thanksgiving let your requests be made known unto God. (KJV)

In nothing be anxious, but in everything, by prayer and petition with thanksgiving, let your requests be made known to God. (WEB)

My Favorite Bible Translation of this Verse:

Pause to Ponder

Doodle . Draw . Write . Doodle . Draw . Write

Who?

What?

When?

Where?

Why?

How?

What if?

1 Peter 5:6-7

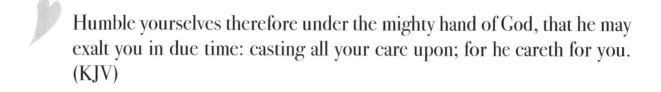

Humble yourselves therefore under the mighty hand of God, that he may exalt you in due time: casting all your care upon; for he careth for you. (KJV)

Humble yourselves therefore under the mighty hand of God, that he may exalt you in due time; casting all your worries on him, because he cares for you. (WEB)

My Favorite Bible Translation of this Verse:

Pause to Ponder

Doodle . Draw . Write . Doodle . Draw . Write

Who?

What?

When?

Where?

Why?

How?

What if?

Psalm 35:1

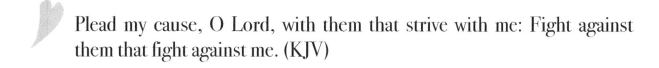 Plead my cause, O Lord, with them that strive with me: Fight against them that fight against me. (KJV)

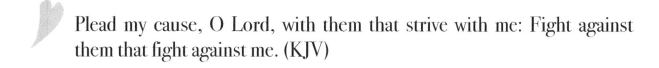 Contend, Yahweh, with those who contend with me. Fight against those who fight against me. (WEB)

My Favorite Bible Translation of this Verse:

Pause to Ponder

Who?

What?

When?

Where?

Why?

How?

What if?

Isaiah 41:10

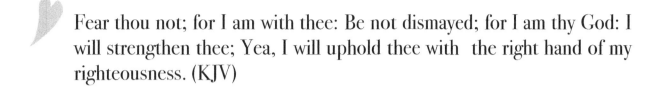 Fear thou not; for I am with thee: Be not dismayed; for I am thy God: I will strengthen thee; Yea, I will uphold thee with the right hand of my righteousness. (KJV)

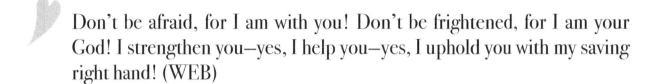 Don't be afraid, for I am with you! Don't be frightened, for I am your God! I strengthen you—yes, I help you—yes, I uphold you with my saving right hand! (WEB)

My Favorite Bible Translation of this Verse:

Pause to Ponder

Doodle . Draw . Write . Doodle . Draw . Write

Who?

What?

When?

Where?

Why?

How?

What if?

Psalm 28:7

The Lord is my strength and my shield; My heart trusted in him, and I was helped: Therefore my heart greatly rejoiceth; And with my song will I praise him. (KJV)

Yahweh is my strength and my shield. My heart has trusted in him, and I am helped. Therefore my heart greatly rejoices. With my song I will thank him. (WEB)

My Favorite Bible Translation of this Verse:

Pause to Ponder

Doodle . Draw . Write . Doodle . Draw . Write

Who?

What?

When?

Where?

Why?

How?

What if?

About the Author / Artist

Debbie Hannah Skinner

Debbie Hannah Skinner is an artist, author, and Bible teacher who delights in helping women engage their hands in art as a way to focus their hearts on God.

She speaks nationally with a Bible in one hand and watercolor brush in the other, painting as she presents to women's groups. Debbie inspires women to paint the world around them with the beautiful colors of hope and help they discover in Scripture.

Debbie especially loves to help women who think they are *non-artists* discover the joy of using watercolor art as a vibrant expression of faith. (Though artists are certainly invited to join in the fun as well!)

Founder of WisdomInWatercolor.com, Debbie specializes in the use of watercolor paints and pencils for Bible journaling, prayer journaling, and Scripture meditation. Her paintings have been published nationally and her prints are available online at her ImageKind gallery.

Visit Debbie's online print gallery:
DebbieHannahSkinner.ImageKind.com

Connect with Debbie at:
WisdomInWatercolor.com

Book Debbie for a Speaking Event or
a Color Through the Bible Workshop:
ChristianSpeakersServices.com/debbiehannahskinner.html

Hope Is Always Near

I love colorful gift books! When I walked through a difficult time as a freshman in college, a friend encouraged me greatly by placing a Scripture-based gift book in my hands one day. From that moment on, creating a gift book became a life dream of mine. "Maybe I could encourage someone someday as well," I thought.

That dream became a reality with the publication of *Hope Is Always Near*.

Hope Is Always Near weaves together Bible verses about hope with accompanying quotes. My paintings serve as the backdrop and there's space to doodle throughout and journal in the back. I hope you find encouragement through *Hope Is Always Near* and that you share it with people you love.
 – Debbie

Hope Is Always Near is a colorful gift book that uses Debbie's words and paintings alongside selected Scriptures to speak to our longing for hope in a world that sometimes feels hopeless.

To order a copy, visit:
WisdomInWatercolor.com/book-store

Stay Connected

Want to know more? To learn about
upcoming volumes of this coloring book series
plus
Debbie's online art classes & other resources,
please visit

ColorThroughTheBible.com

Website: WisdomInWatercolor.com
Facebook: ColorThroughTheBibleScriptureSavors

Play Ground

Use this area to test your markers or colors before applying them to a page.

Made in the USA
Coppell, TX
06 September 2020